The Sugar Cube

Little hint of sweetness in disguise.

Suraksha

ISBN 978-93-5458-570-8
© Suraksha 2021
Published in India 2021 by Pencil

A brand of
One Point Six Technologies Pvt. Ltd.
123, Building J2, Shram Seva Premises,
Wadala Truck Terminal, Wadala (E)
Mumbai 400037, Maharashtra, INDIA
E connect@thepencilapp.com
W www.thepencilapp.com

Author biography

They say "you don't know you're strong
until you've been through the worst and have won".
But what if I always believed that I was strong.
That I believed no matter what may come,
giving up was never on my list.
That I was ready to face lonely nights,
and betrayal down the street.
That I faced criticism and injustice
and yet kept on going.
But I also cry when I don't get enough words
to explain exactly what I want to say.
That my pillows carry the floods flowed down my eyes
and when my mother is far away.

The author comes from a family of four, her parents her brother and herself. She completed her higher studies from St. Joseph's international residential school, sriperumbudur,Tamil Nadu. Right now she's pursuing her higher studies from Andaman and Nicobar Islands Institute of Medical Sciences - ANIIMS,says she writes to calm her chaos and this is her very first selfie authored book with her past work in 3 anthologies. She's looking forward to do better in this field with better outputs some day.

This book sugar cube, contains pages carrying weight heavier than our school bags. It carries the weight of the struggles, the lessons learned and the very words I needed to hear the most to bring me contentment in times of need and hence, the sugar cube, a little hint of sweetness in disguise.

CONTENTS

Foreword

This book holds the words, that one needs when they're at the lowest points of their life. The words one craves to hear to be guided along the journey, to know that they are loved and cares about. The author felt these were the words she needed to hear to find comfort, because writing these down calmed her chaos. These pages hold the weight of all the struggles and storms, the lessons learned and the tears shed in the authors' life. Hope it's calms your chaotic soul.

Things go back

Things go back to where they come from.
Nature has the motion set in proof and
that's how life happens too.
And I hope that in this one life that you've got,
may you be the house from where all good things fliw
so that at the end of the day, they find their way back to
you.

Pull you down

Even though what we need to embrace is
helping nature and kindness,
but about what the world has turned into,
makes me want to say,
be sure ofwhom you are lending a hand to.
Sometimes they might just pull you down to get back up,
and when you hand a place so good to someone with such
a bad soul, you're not just doing bad to your own,
but to yourself, your place and to every other good soul
who believed you could do better.
Don't ever let that happen.

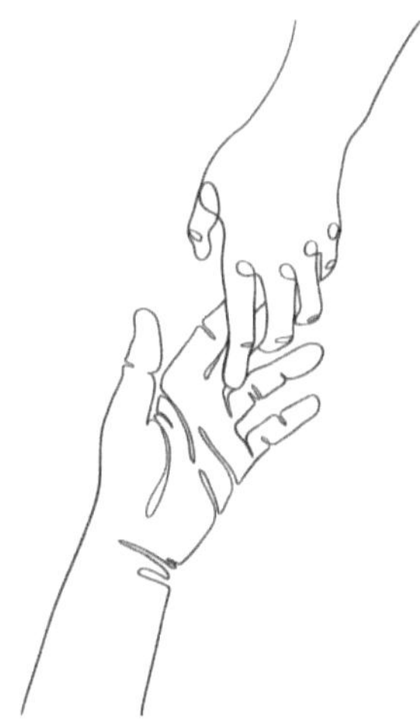

Keep going

You need peace to keep going in life
and to do better, and when you do better
you inspire people to do better, and at this point,
you're doing your best.
There's nothing better than making people
wanting to keep going in life and a will to do better
every new day.

Grounded

I hope you find enough achievements
to keep you flying high but
enough failures in life
to keep you grounded.
I hope you never forget where you came from.
The day you do, you will lose yourself forever.

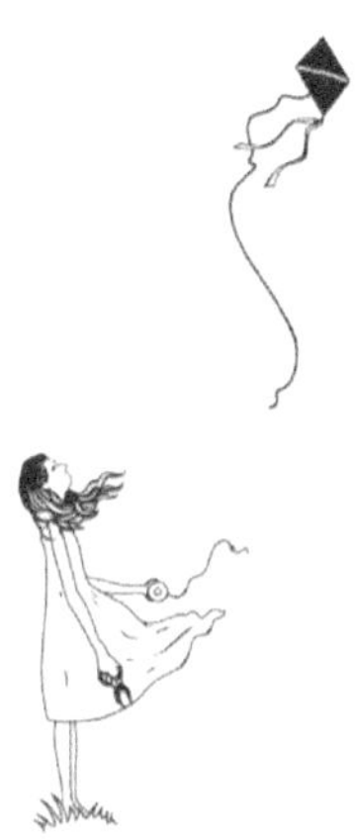

My flaws

The demons in my head knew,
that I would commit mistakes,
over and over again,
that fast learning was not my thing,
that I would bleed a hundred times,
just to understand one wound,
that I will break rules,
despite of knowing the consequences,
and still ask for forgiveness,
like I owe it.
That I'm filled with flaws,
and may be till the end a part of me,
will always be defined by my grave mistakes.
But the angel inside me knows
the things I've been through,
the strings I had to pull just to keep going,
that the other side of the river has always been,
too far than just on the other side,
that I had chances to give up but I didn't.
And so today, I choose this angel in me over the demon
that I choose to believe that I'm a creation of that almighty
who is, perfectly flawed to do imperfections and yet never
gives up,
over the demon who keeps saying that,
I'll always be a worthless person.

If taking in good, helps you bring out the good,
then why choose bad.
You owe yourself better darling.

The pain never gets better

They say you know you're healed,
when you don't cry over the same thing again.
I think, at one point we all stop crying,
but I don't think everything heals.
Evolution is a part of what we are,
and eventually we all learn to live,
With the thorns,
amongst the roses in our very own hearts.
Does their pricking pain any lesser?
I don't think so.
Do we all someday learn to cope?
Yes we do.
The pain doesn't get any better,
Yet through the course of time,
we all learn not feed our pain with tears.

When I was two

I wish I could cherish and love this life,
like I did when I was two.
Effortlessly, unknowingly.
Like how beautiful it felt just to run free beneath those branches,
to be able to hold hands with friends and sing songs in circles.
Oh how I danced on hearing the sound of ice cream van,
Of being chased my mom for breaking my toys,
and being saved by dad from all my punishments.
e best part was always, being tired after a beautiful day
and falling into the arms of sleep without worrying about tomorrow.

One tear at a time

Their words cut deep.
You could barely breathe that night.
Your throat might ache of the words you've
suppressed because they reply with
the rudest of words.
Your stomach aches,
for you want to shout out loud,
but you can't.
I know how it feels in your veins,
that depression creeping in.
But love only if you knew,
how strong you are.
Let it all in, even if it breaks you,
so it finds the door to leave from where it entered,
and take a long breath with your eyes closed,
you will slowly heal if you believe,
one tear at a time.

The place I belong

I may not be where I'm supposed to be,
but may be that place isn't so far.
May be all my hardwork today,
will take me there tomorrow or a day after.
May be it's not as far as I thought it would be.
May be it's that building where the road ends,
or the valley on the other side of my house.
May be it's near the shop down the road where,
I loved to take a sip of tea, or may it's across the lake
or may be it's just a head turn away.
It may not be as far as I fear,
but it also may not be as close as I hope.
But I sure know that one day all these works of mine
will be paid off,
and I'll be taken there, to that beautiful place.
where I belong.

The ugliest Thing

Sometimes the ugliest things
aren't people and places.
Sometimes it's our mind itself,
yes, the ugliest thing.
Always taking us back to the ruins,
we've been in an illusion of running away from,
over and over again.

The grief will be over

All the grief will be over someday.
Nothing bad in this world has ever been
so fortunate enough to last forever unless
you give them the power to do so.
So my dear, may you find solace
in knowing that all of this will be over soon
and you'll be alright.
That a better day will soon be on the horizon.
That all the grief will not be for nothing
and you will grow through everything that's been
aching through your bones.
All those unspoken pains will be worth it.
And trust me, you will be better tomorrow.

Define you

Let no deceit, pain, destructive thought,
and anything filthy come from you.
Make your heart a beautiful place
for people to visit.
Let nothing evil come from you.
You owe yourself a beautiful soul
and a gentle heart.
Let strong, fierce, bold yet kind and every other
beautiful word define your very self.

Life

May you catch the essence of this life
at the very corners you stopped by
to catch a breath.
At the corridor, near the staircase,
on the swing, under the tree,
and while driving through the beauty of nature.
Life passes in a blink of eyes and
may that millisecond mean more than
what you have just barely seen.
May that essence reach you skin deep
and heal all the scars you've hidden
for so long till this very moment.

Growth

I have heard them say
"walk the hallways like you own the place".
What I wish to say is,
walk the hallway like no one owns that place.
Like you have been placed in a whole new world.
Take adventures, hurt and heal, fall and rise,
and just keep going.
For there's growth in learning and
growth is all we need to get through this life.
A growth of self, to accompany us
through our very own hardships.

Bloom again

When you're in your room
and the shadow of that tree falls on your curtains
with the lights shinning by
passing through the spaces between the leaves
and somehow making it's way to your window,
I want you to know that tomorrow will be a better day.
It may not seem so today, but soon enough it will.
It doesn't rain forever.
Eventually the wind comes in
and drives the dark clouds away.
Since the earth rotates, the weather is ought to change
and since life revolves,
our seasons are ought to change too
and we will survive like those flowers in the garden
and bloom when the sun shines again.

My pillows

They soaked all my tears,
heard all my cries.
Knew all my wins,
failure and trials.
I was searching for support,
and found it in my arms.
The comfort I thus find
and all my chaos calms.

I will Fly

On a fine day,
when the right moment arrives,
I'm going to get rid off the suffocation.
I will not feel that pain anymore,
and the shell shall break,
and my wings shall grow,
and I'll fly like a butterfly out of the cocoon
that suffocated me but also remained always
a shelter for my growth.

Bottling up

Everytime you criticize someone
for what they've been in past
forgetting that you know these
because they chose you to open up to
because they had better thoughts about you
than who you are, only teaches them never to
open up themselves and thus they remain bottled up
with all their emotions, one of the main reasons
why we find so many souks wasted hanging from ceilings
and overdosed veins, wrist bleeds and unending pains.

To all the Christians out there

Even the Son of God had to meet his fate.
To be nailed up on the cross for our sins.
Then who are we to fight and complain about the fate
we've got in our life.
We sin endlessly forgetting to repent has made it clear
that we don't deserve to complain about anything.
We being able to eat, have a shelter,
and able to wake up to a new day
is a greater blessing in itself that we'll always fail to
understand
until the the day to pay comes up.

You keep getting better

You keep getting better when you learn to
embrace your flaws,
learn from your past,
compete yourself from who you were,
and help others to ride as you rise along
knowing you alone getting better
doesn't make the world a better place.
One flower blooming doesn't turn
a grassland into garden,
but when all bloom together,
it's looks nothing lesser than what we call heavenly.

The one who stands by you

The people who always stood by you,
may risk their life for your well being and
may you never underestimate the extent
they'd go for you.
You might just end up making
the worst mistake of your life.

Age

After we grow we wished
that we knew our worth
since our birth
that we are complete and perfectly flawed
to be cherished at every step of our life.
But we only learn these with the lessons
life throws at us, age being the criteria for
when we have to face, the reason some of us
has had a lot at a very young age
and some of us are still lost
even at 30.

Humbleness

Nobody who ever succeeded is ahead of you
and nobody who ever failed is behind you.
All are walking life at their own pace
and are placed where they need to be.
I think pride is something we must never
let our hearts be ruled by.
And humbleness is a necessity to be cultivated.

Moment

Our life is nothing but a moment.
Some of us have the privilege of having this moment last for 70 years and some limited to a day.
I hope all of us, no matter the length, have something beautiful to remember, when the last day of this moment finally arrives at our doorstep.

Heartwarming beautiful things

In our race of being able to succeed to
live a life in a beautiful city with luxury and comfort
has kept us so busy that we forget the lasting peace little things
from remote countryside places leaves us with.
A simple breeze at the shore, the sound of air passing between the trees, the sound of birds at the sunrise, and the waves coming back to its heights when the sun sets.
Sipping tea in a small shop when it rains heavy and the sound
of people you love around you.
We forget all these heartwarming beautiful things, however in this busy life ours, we always end up craving for these little yet great things unknowingly at the little corner of our hearts.

Phoenix

If you think you're born with a fate of failure,
you also need to learn that you're blessed with
the strength of the Phoenix,
to rise up from the ashes of the same fire
that brought you down.
You possess this strength
you'll never know if you never try
to rise up every time you fall.

Stronger creation

You are astronger creation of the almighty.

Embrace your strength of facing all the vulnerabilities and pain.

Woman, your pelvis carries the terrible pain every month and holds the magic of giving birth to a new life. You're stronger than you think. Just because someone says you're a weaker gender, doesn't hold the strength of making such a strong creation weaker. Remember this wherever you go.

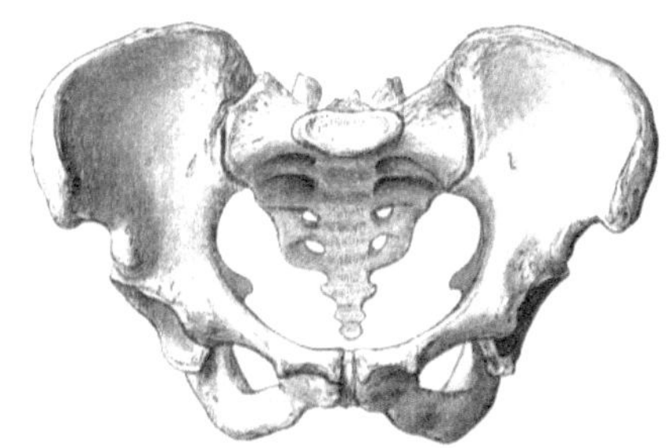

Own your mistakes

You blaming others for your mistakes
will never give you peace. It will grow as a fire inside you
to destroy you. We're all imperfect and so do we all
commit certain mistakes in life. Own your mistakes. Best
parts are easy to accept but accepting our worst parts is
what makes us capable of fighting through hard times, for
it is then that you finally realize who you are and how
much you are capable of.

Mirror

We look at ourselves in the mirror
and consider ourselves disgraced for the things we don't have
instead of being content and happy to be whatever we are with whatever we have.

Her shades

She laughed in various colours of crayons
shed her tears in shades of blues
her suffering coded beautiful grey
and all her shades were true.

Notes

To all my readers, never underestimate the power you carry under under your skin. You're beautiful, strong and powerful. Take care of yourself.